D1586411

Why We Should
Go Vegan

Magnus Vinding

First edition

Copyright © 2014 Magnus Vinding

ISBN: 1496069919
ISBN-13: 978-1496069917

CONTENTS

INTRODUCTION

Why should we go vegan? In short, because it is the only ethically defensible thing to do. It would significantly increase the well-being of conscious creatures, including human well-being, if humanity went vegan, and that is exactly what we ultimately should strive toward: *to maximize the well-being of sentient beings*.

That going vegan would generally be much better both for us humans and our fellow sentient creatures seems like a rather bombastic claim to make, and one that requires a good deal of justification. The goal of this short book is to provide this justification – to present the relevant facts, and to point out how these facts so clearly reveal that we should go vegan. It should be noted here that what is meant by going vegan in this context is to abstain from eating meat (including meat from poultry and fish), dairy and eggs, which is what this book focuses on. It is in this sense the word 'vegan' is used here.

I actually think that the question about whether we should go vegan or not is one of the easiest ethical questions to answer at this point in time, and I even think that most people would agree if they were only presented with detailed information about the consequences of our not being vegan. Presently, our view is clouded by two things: the first is tradition and the other is our failure to see the consequences of our actions. Together, these two make up the thick cloud that prevents us from seeing that our practice of raising and eating animals is morally reprehensible.

That our practice of raising and eating animals is atrocious may sound absurd and extreme to most people – I would surely have felt so myself a few years ago – but this is only because we have not dared to really question

2

and scrutinize our own tradition; we have not thought deeply about what it is that we do and the possible alternatives we have. The mistake we make is that we take the broad consensus of our peers to be the gold standard of moral wisdom. As history shows, and as a closer examination of the current consensus on moral issues reveals, that view is clearly mistaken. What we all consider to be ethically justifiable is not necessarily justifiable at all. We must look to reason, not tradition, in order to find out what we should and should not do. So what we need to do is simply to question our tradition and consensus, and to put the relevant facts and reasons on the table.

WE DO NOT NEED ANYTHING FROM ANIMALS FOR OUR HEALTH

It is a common myth that we need to eat animals or anything that comes from animals in order to be healthy. The truth is that we don't. All that we know today about nutrition points clearly toward that we can have optimal health without eating animals or anything from animals at all, and this has been expressed clearly by numerous professional dietitians and scientists working in the field of nutrition.[1] Here is for instance the position of what is now known as the Academy of Nutrition and Dietetics (known as American Dietetic Association before 2012), which is the largest organization of nutrition experts in the United States:

It is the position of the American Dietetic Association that appropriately planned vegetarian diets, including total vegetarian or vegan diets, are healthful, nutritionally adequate, and may provide health benefits in the prevention and treatment of certain diseases. Well-planned vegetarian diets are appropriate for individuals during all stages of the life cycle, including pregnancy, lactation, infancy, childhood, and adolescence, and for athletes.[2]

So now we have the first relevant fact on the table: We do not need to consume anything that comes from animals in order to be healthy. What we do need in order to be healthy on a vegan diet, however, is to supplement our diet with vitamin B12 (and, needless to say, to eat a *healthy* vegan diet – to eat nuts, legumes and green leafy vegetables instead of white bread, chips and cookies). Vitamin B12 is produced by bacteria, and since we very wisely have limited our intake of dirt that could provide us with such bacteria and vitamin B12 by washing our vegetables and by cleaning the water we drink, we have to take vitamin B12 supplements in order to get it in a vegan diet.

Another thing that vegans, along with most other people, may also want to supplement their diet with is omega-3 DHA and EPA fatty acids, which may promote good cardiovascular health, a well-functioning nervous system and good mental health, and it may even help slow down aging.[3] These fatty acids are found in algae, and they can be bought as algae oil capsules that are at least as good as meat from "oily fish" as a source of omega-3.[4] And, unlike shellfish and fish meat, these capsules do not contain any mercury, which is highly toxic – especially for our brains, and the link between intake of meat from certain kinds of fish and diminished cognitive ability has also been well-documented.[5] As one study reported: "[For consumption of meat from certain predator species of fish] a negative effect up to 10 points on the IQ score was found."[6] And, unlike many kinds of omega-3 capsules with fish oil, including many, perhaps even all, of those that are branded as "PCB-free", algae omega-3 capsules actually are PCB-free.[7] These facts about fish meat, fish oil capsules and algae oil capsules suggest that algae oil capsules are the safest source of these fatty acids.

Another widespread myth is that it is hard to get enough protein from a vegan diet, which is again just plain wrong. Nuts, seeds and lentils contain high amounts of protein in terms of weight, and even bread and oats contain quite high amounts of protein too. In fact, what is hard is to *not* get enough protein, on any diet, because it is quite hard to avoid protein, which makes it a mystery how this myth has ever become so widespread. Again: We can easily have all our nutritional needs met on a vegan diet.

Not only do we not need to eat meat, dairy or eggs in order to be healthy, but much actually seems to suggest that abstaining from eating this could help us become even more healthy than otherwise, and help us prevent many instances of death. Red meat – meat from cows, pigs and sheep – has for instance been found to increase mortality risk significantly. As one study found:

> After multivariate adjustment for major lifestyle and dietary risk factors, the pooled hazard ratio (HR) (95% CI) of total mortality for a 1-serving-per-day increase was 1.13 (1.07-1.20) for unprocessed red meat and 1.20 (1.15-1.24) for processed red meat.[8]

So for each increase of just a single serving of red meat a day, the mortality risk seems to increase with about 13-20 percent, which is rather significant. It was also estimated in this study that respectively 9.3 and 7.6 percent of the deaths in men and women that had been observed by the end of the study could have been prevented had all the subjects been eating significantly less red meat.[9] The conclusions of this study were summed up in the following way:

Red meat consumption [consumption of cow meat, pig meat and sheep meat] is associated with an increased risk of total, CVD [cardiovascular disease], and cancer mortality. Substitution of other healthy protein sources for red meat is associated with a lower mortality risk.[10]

In contrast, consumption of the perhaps most obvious alternative source of protein, namely legumes – beans, lentils, peanuts, peas, chick peas etc. – seems to be linked to longevity and reduced mortality risk. As a study that was undertaken among five cohorts in different parts of the world concluded: "[...] the legume food group showed 7-8% reduction in mortality hazard ratio for every 20g increase in daily intake [...]"[11] So 20 grams of legumes seems to be about half as good as a serving of red meat seems to be bad. It seems that if we want to live longer and healthier lives, we should replace meat with legumes as our main source of protein (and of course be physically active, get good sleep and not smoke).

But should we merely decrease our intake of meat and eat it in moderation, or should we stop eating it altogether in order to live as long and healthy lives as possible? One meta-study seems to give a tentative hint, as it found a "very low meat intake" to be associated with increased longevity, while the data from one cohort "raised the possibility" that a long-term adherence (more than 20 years) to a diet totally devoid of any kind of meat can "[...] further produce a significant 3.6-y increase in life expectancy."[12] But nothing implied that eating a small amount of meat was in any way better than eating no meat at all.[13]

It is not just consumption of red meat (linked to increased mortality risk) and consumption of shellfish and fish meat (increases the mercury-levels in our body) that have certain adverse effects on our health that we can avoid by eating a vegan diet, but also consumption of poultry meat, eggs and dairy.

Chicken meat – especially from "conventional chicken" – for instance contains high amounts of arsenic,[14] and intake of arsenic should, like intake of mercury, be minimized:

> Arsenic is a human carcinogen, and is also associated with increased risks of several noncancer endpoints, including cardio-vascular disease, diabetes, neuropathy, and neurocognitive deficits in children.[15]

High arsenic-levels might also be part of the reason why consumption of poultry meat has been associated with various types of cancer, such as B-cell lymphomas and follicular lymphomas.[16]

Chicken meat is also one of the most bacteria-filled kinds of meat we eat. A recent study from Consumer Report for instance found that 97 percent of the hundreds of samples of chicken meat they tested contained dangerous bacteria.[17] 80 percent contained the bacteria enterococcus, which can cause bladder infections and meningitis, 65 percent contained the fecal contaminant E. coli and 11 percent contained salmonella. Furthermore, the study also found very high levels of bacteria resistant to antibiotics that pose a huge challenge to modern medicine and public health.[18] It is tempting to ask why we want to make this challenge much harder than it needs to be by eating meat that we do not need for our health.

When it comes to eggs, various connections have been made between consumption of eggs and suboptimal health. One study for instance found that consuming just a single egg a day increases mortality risk significantly: "[the study found] an adjusted hazard ratio of 1.41 for all-cause mortality over a 20-y span in 21.327 Harvard-educated male physicians who ate ≥1 egg/d."[19] What explains such a significant increase in mortality risk – about the same increase that smoking 1-2 cigarettes a day causes – is probably to a great extend the high amounts of LDL cholesterol found in eggs. Another study found that even just a single egg a week seems to increase the risk of type 2 diabetes with 76 percent, while consuming a single egg a day more than tripled this risk.[20]

There are also very compelling reasons to stay away from dairy products, especially if one is prone to acne, since studies have found dairy intake to be highly associated with acne.[21] It is not only acne that consumption of dairy products, particularly the hormones they contain, seems to cause, but also breast and prostate cancer.[22] As one study concluded:

The evidence assembled here suggests that dairy-sourced hormones, not being subject to any innate feedback inhibition, may be the source of the androgenic and mitogenic progestins that drive acne, prostate and breast cancer. This is the most promising unitary hypothesis available to explain the etiology of diverse diseases that blemish, scar, shorten and take the lives of millions.[23]

Another good reason to minimize our consumption of animal parts and things derived from animals in general is the amount of highly toxic PCB's that are found in them. As one study found:

> In food, the highest mean contamination level was observed in fish and fish derived products followed by eggs, milk and their products, and meat and meat products from terrestrial animals. The lowest contamination was observed in foods of plant origin.[24]

Of all things, fish oils were found to have the highest contamination levels. Yet another reason we might want to avoid feeding our children with animal flesh and things from animals is that consumption of animal protein in childhood has been linked to a significantly earlier onset of puberty compared to consumption of vegetable protein, and earlier puberty is linked to increased rates of cancer and a shorter lifespan.[25] It is, however, not only children who may benefit from eating vegan protein instead of animal protein, but people of all ages, since vegan protein intake in general seems to reduce the risk of many types of cancer. As one study, titled "Vegan proteins may reduce risk of cancer, obesity, and cardiovascular disease by promoting increased glucagon activity", concluded:

[Vegans tend to have] decreased risk for certain prominent 'Western' cancers; a vegan diet has documented clinical efficacy in rheumatoid arthritis. Low-fat vegan diets may be especially protective in regard to cancers linked to insulin resistance--namely, breast and colon cancer--as well as prostate cancer; conversely, the high IGF-I activity associated with heavy ingestion of animal products may be largely responsible for the epidemic of 'Western' cancers in wealthy societies.[26]

So far we have seen that many negative effects are linked to consumption of meat, dairy and eggs, but is there any evidence that suggests that an entirely plant-based diet would be better for us overall? As we shall now see, a lot actually does seem to imply that a healthy vegan diet could help us improve human health overall, and help us prevent many of the diseases we presently suffer and die from.

One of our greatest epidemics today is obesity. It is estimated that more than 500 million people suffer from obesity worldwide today, and that it kills more than three million people each year. In comparison, about 55,000 people are killed in war each year, which of course in no way suggests that we are overestimating the horror and seriousness of war – how could we? – but the little attention we give to obesity in comparison does suggest, however, that we are not taking the "war" we should be waging against obesity seriously. It seems that we overlook what a merciless killer and cause of pain that obesity and the overeating that leads to it really is: it increases the risk of heart disease (the most common cause of death worldwide), many kinds of cancer, type 2 diabetes, degenerative joint disease and mental problems such as depression and low self-esteem.[27] Fortunately, a lot seems to imply that we have a very powerful and peaceful weapon at our hands that can help us overcome obesity: a vegan diet.

Various studies have pointed quite clearly toward a vegan diet as a promising way to overcome obesity, and toward consumption of meat, eggs and dairy as being a significant contributing cause of our obesity epidemic. One study for instance looked at the BMI of more than 60,000 people and found that people averagely had a significantly lower BMI the "closer" they were to eating a vegan diet:

Mean BMI was lowest in vegans (23.6) and incrementally higher in lacto-ovo vegetarians (25.7), pesco-vegetarians (26.3), semi-vegetarians (27.3), and non-vegetarians (28.8).[28]

So only among vegans was the average BMI below the range that is considered overweight (25-30), and among the so-called non-vegetarians, the BMI was more than 5 BMI-units higher than among the vegans. One might expect this significant difference to be at least partly attributable to a more active lifestyle among vegans compared to non-vegetarians, but that is not the case, since the non-vegetarians were actually *more* physically active. Furthermore, the study also found that a vegan diet decreased the risk of getting type 2 diabetes significantly – even after "lifestyle characteristics and BMI were taken into account" – but this should not be surprising since we know that consumption of eggs significantly increases the risk of getting type 2 diabetes, and studies have also suggested that consumption of cheese and meat increases this risk too.[29]

Another big study followed more than 370,000 people over more than five years and found consumption of meat – both red meat and poultry meat – to be linked to weight gain over this period of five years. The perhaps most significant and surprising finding of this study was that even after controlling for caloric intake, eating meat was still associated with greater weight gain compared to a diet with the same amount of calories, but with a lower intake of meat.[30]

So it seems that, even after controlling for physical activity and caloric intake, a diet with meat makes us gain more weight than a vegan diet, which may be a large part of the explanation why vegans generally seem to be much leaner than meat eaters. Given the above-mentioned findings, it seems very likely that consumption of meat, eggs and dairy is a significant contributing cause of our obesity epidemic, and that a vegan diet could help us overcome it – again, 23.6 vs. 28.8 in average BMI is a big difference, especially given the fact that the vegans were not more physically active than those who ate animals and things from animals. A lot therefore seems to suggest that the global adoption of a vegan diet could help us save thousands of lives annually, and also help us cut down the economic costs of obesity, which, according to one estimate, is more than 200 billion dollars annually in the US alone.[31]

Aside from obesity, a plant-based diet also seems likely to help us overcome many other diseases and conditions. For instance, one study that followed more than 27,000 people of which more than half did not eat meat found that after adjusting for both age, smoking and education, those who did not eat meat had a significantly lower risk of multiple conditions and diseases such as coronary heart disease, stroke, high blood pressure, diabetes, diverticulosis, rheumatoid arthritis and rheumatism.[32] Another big study looked at data from more than 70,000 people and found a diet devoid of meat to be "associated with lower all-cause mortality" and concluded that: "These favorable associations should be considered carefully by those offering dietary guidance."[33]

It is not just our physical health that a plant-based diet seems helpful for, however, since there are also tentative hints that it can be helpful for our mental health. One study set out to examine whether a diet without meat would have adverse effects on people's mood, and it actually found the opposite to be the case, since, on average, those who ate no meat "reported significantly less negative emotion than omnivores [...]"[34] Another study that followed omnivores who had to stop eating meat and eggs for a period of time echoed this conclusion: "The complete restriction of flesh foods significantly reduced mood variability in omnivores."[35] It is not clear why not consuming meat and eggs seems to have a positive effect on mood, but it may be because of the arachidonic acid that is prevalent in eggs and meat, especially poultry meat.[36]

Based on what we have seen so far, we can make the following general conclusion in relation to nutrition: We do not need to consume animals or anything that comes from animals in order to be healthy, and our consumption of animal flesh, eggs and dairy is in fact bad for our health in many ways.

IT WOULD BE BETTER FOR HUMANITY

The conclusion that we do not need to consume anything that comes from animals in order to be healthy is important in relation to whether we should keep on or stop eating animals, eggs and dairy for the sake of humanity. It allows us to move on from the nutritional perspective, from which – as has just been made clear – there is no positive case for our practice of raising animals, and to look at the other consequences that our raising, killing and eating animals has for humanity. Because if the other consequences of this are largely negative for us, then we clearly should stop this practice for the sake of humanity. As we shall now see, this is indeed the case.[37]

A consequence of our practice of raising and eating animals that seems widely overlooked, or at least not taken seriously, is that it increases the risk and prevalence of fatal diseases and epidemics among humans – it needlessly kills countless human beings every year. Many of the terrible diseases that have caused suffering and death upon humans throughout history have been so-called zoonotic diseases that we got from animals we farmed and/or ate. These are diseases such as those caused by H1N1-viruses (responsible for the 1918 flu pandemic that is estimated to have infected 500 million people and killed 50-100 million people – at least 10 million more than were killed during the First World War – and the 2009 swine flu that killed hundreds of thousands of people, and both these pandemics are thought to have originated from farm herds of birds and pigs), HIV (estimated to have killed 35 million people and to have infected twice as many; the most plausible explanation of how HIV arose is that it is a mutated form of a virus that was transmitted to humans from apes killed and eaten in Central Africa in the early 20th century, which shows the fatal risks related to eating so-called "exotic meat"), H5N1-viruses, and other diseases like SARS, Salmonellosis (salmonella infection), Creutzfeldt-Jakob disease, Newcastle disease, hog cholera, Lassa fever, Ebola, and the list goes on.

We are really gambling with our lives by farming animals, because we cannot effectively guard ourselves against such diseases, and we cannot know when or where the next outbreak will happen or how deadly it will be. And such outbreaks happen all the time; for instance recently, in 2013, an influenza outbreak was caused by the virus H7N9 that spread from farm animals to humans. This outbreak reportedly "only" killed 48 people, but it could have killed millions of people had certain mutations happened in the virus, and we cannot guard ourselves against the occurrence of such mutations in the animals we raise, and we in fact only provide ideal conditions for the spread of viruses when we squeeze thousands of animals tightly together in dirty halls. What we *can* do, however, is that we can minimize the risk of the occurrence of these mutations drastically, which can be done by minimizing the number of animals we raise and slaughter completely down to zero, because the fewer animals we raise, the smaller is the risk that new diseases arise and mutate in animals and spread to human beings.

It is hard to overstate how big a problem the animals we farm are for human health, because it is no small amount of human diseases that come from animals:

A remarkable 61 percent of all human pathogens, and 75 percent of new human pathogens, are transmitted by animals, and some of the most lethal bugs affecting humans originate in our domesticated animals.[38]

The suffering and death of humans from diseases that spread from farm animals alone makes quite a clear case that we should, for the sake of humans, stop our needless practice of raising and eating animals, since we can avoid these deaths in this way, as we could have avoided millions of deaths that diseases like AIDS and avian flus have demanded had we stopped eating and farming animals earlier – we could have prevented loss of human lives in numbers comparable to, maybe even greater than, the number of lives lost in the two world wars. Our practice of raising and eating animals unnecessarily increases the risk of dangerous diseases, and it unnecessarily kills human beings. It lies in our hands now to collectively take the appropriate action that will save innumerable human lives: to stop farming and eating animals.

The economic costs of the diseases that have spread from animals we farmed or killed, and the economic costs of animal farming in general, only adds to the incentive to abandon our practice of farming animals. For instance, more than 10 billion dollars have been spent alone on preventing the H5N1-virus from infecting and killing people, and such an expense, along with the more than 400 billion dollars that it is estimated that so-called "animal food production" imposes on society in the United States alone, makes a strong economic case for abandoning the farming of animals for the sake of humans, since these billions of dollars surely could have been spent better on human beings otherwise.[39]

Another problem with animal farming in relation to human health and life is that our animal farm practices are undermining the effectiveness of our hard-won weapons against bacterial infections: antibiotics. Antibiotics have saved millions of lives since they were first discovered in the first half of the 20th century, but their effectiveness is unfortunately declining as a natural consequence of our use of them. When we fight bacteria with antibiotics, we naturally promote the growth of the bacteria that can withstand the antibiotics best – they become more and more prevalent. So in this way we gradually breed bacteria that are more and more resistant to antibiotics the more we use antibiotics – we are arming them to resist our best weapons. This we have already done to a great degree: A recent estimate is that, in the United States alone, at least two million people become sick every year because of bacteria that are resistant to antibiotics, and at least 23,000 of them die from their infection, which, as a point of comparison, makes these antibiotic-resistant bacteria a problem that is more than twice as big as firearm-related homicides in the United States in terms of annual deaths. [40]

So what have these resistant bacteria got to do with the animals we raise to be eaten? A lot, because we feed farm animals with enormous amounts of antibiotics. In the United States, for instance, about 80 percent of all the antibiotics used are given to farm animals – much of which is not even given for medical purposes but for the purpose of promoting faster growth in the animals.[41] Again, the more antibiotics we use, the more antibiotic-resistant bacteria will evolve, which increases the risk that bacterial infections will make us seriously sick and kill us, since our treatments then become less effective.

The problems that follow from our use of antibiotics in farm animals are widely recognized as serious and hard to find solutions to – after all, if we do not feed our farm animals with antibiotics, we will increase the risk that the animals carry salmonella and other dangerous bacteria that can also infect humans. It seems that we are facing a hard problem here. Fortunately, we do actually have a complete solution at our hands that will solve all the problems that are related to this hard problem, and which thereby very likely will prevent thousands of human deaths from antibiotic-resistant bacteria every year, namely to stop raising animals in the first place. Unfortunately, this solution is both widely overlooked and dismissed since it goes radically against our traditions. Again, our attachment to eating animals is needlessly killing human beings.

What we have seen so far – that our raising and eating of animals needlessly causes suffering and death for thousands of human beings every year – reveals, indeed quite clearly, that we have an obligation to all our fellow human beings (since we are *all* exposed to this increased risk of disease and death in today's interconnected global human society) and to ourselves to not support the raising of farm animals in any way, and even to help us stop it completely. This may sound very radical and extreme, and while it sure is radical, it is in no way extreme. We need to wake up to the fact that our raising of farm animals – something we are collectively supporting by buying and eating meat, eggs and dairy – is causing needless human death; that we can prevent thousands, perhaps even millions, of instances of disease and death *every year* if we stop raising farm animals. Indeed, what is both extreme, in-defensible and unbelievable is our indifference and inaction in relation to all this needless human misery and death.

Another alarming aspect of animal farming is the environmental consequences it has, which of course also impact us humans and our future. First of all, livestock "production" is estimated to be responsible for more humanly caused greenhouse gas emissions than any other single source of greenhouse gas emissions (humanly caused because we humans obviously are the ones who have brought livestock "production" into existence). A UN-report estimated that 18 percent of our greenhouse gas emissions, measured in so-called carbon dioxide equi-valents, are caused by livestock, while another study found it to be at least 51 percent.[42] No matter what the exact percentage is, we can be sure that it is significant, and it seems that if we want to cut down on our emissions of green-house gases as drastically as we can, which it increasingly seems we urgently should, we should completely phase out our raising of farm animals, since we could start doing this from today if we collectively chose to.

The UN-report also concluded that: "Livestock are also responsible for almost two-thirds (64 percent) of anthropogenic ammonia emissions, which contribute significantly to acid rain and acidification of ecosystems." – and that: "[The environmental impact of livestock] is so significant that it needs to be addressed with urgency. Major reductions in impact could be achieved at reasonable cost."[43]

Raising livestock is also a very inefficient way to feed our growing human population. One study that looked at the sustainability of meat-based and plant-based diets estimated that it takes 2.3 kilograms of grain in order to get a single kilogram of chicken meat, 3.8 kilograms of grain to get a kilogram of turkey meat, 5.9 kilograms of grain to get a kilogram of pig meat, 11 kilograms of grain in order to get a kilogram of eggs, 13 kilograms of grain and 30 kilograms of forage to get a kilogram of cow meat, and 21 kilograms of grain and 30 kilograms of forage to get a kilogram of sheep meat. This study also estimated the ratio of the energy we spend to the energy we get from some of the things we eat: 57:1 for sheep meat, 40:1 for cow meat, 39:1 for eggs, 14:1 for both pig meat and dairy, 10:1 for turkey meat, 4:1 for chicken meat, and 1:4 for corn.[44] This is also part of the reason why the carbon footprint of meat is generally far higher than that of vegetables: 39.2 kilograms of carbon-dioxide for a kilogram of sheep meat (which corresponds to the carbon footprint of driving 145 kilometers in an average car), 27 kilograms for a kilogram of cow meat, 13.5 for a kilogram of cheese, 12.1 for a kilogram of pig meat, 6.9 for a kilogram of chicken meat, 6.1 for a kilogram of tuna meat, 4.8 for a kilogram of eggs compared to 2.2 for vegetables, 1.1 for fruit and 0.9 for lentils. The organization Foodwatch has estimated that the carbon footprint of a non-organic vegan diet is only 13 percent of the carbon footprint of a non-organic diet with meat, and that the carbon footprint of an organic vegan diet is less than seven percent of that of an organic diet with meat, while it is 13 percent – less than one seventh – of the carbon footprint of an organic vegetarian diet. [45]

Also when it comes to the water that is required it is generally far more wasteful to get a kilogram of animal meat than to get grains, fruits and vegetables. For instance, a kilogram of cow meat requires more than 15,000 liters, sheep meat more than 10,000 liters, pig meat more than 6,000, chicken meat more than 4000, and in comparison it takes around 1,600 liters to produce a kilogram of bread, 800 liters to produce a kilogram of apples or bananas, and 200 to produce a kilogram of tomatoes.[46] In light of all these facts it is not surprising that the end conclusion of the above-mentioned study of the sustainability of meat-based and plant-based diets was that the average meat-based American diet is not sustainable in the long term, and that even the average vegetarian diet, although being more sustainable, is not sustainable in the long term either.[47]

There seems to be a growing concern among many people that we human beings are overpopulating our earth, and that our earth cannot sustain so many of us. Presently we are seven billion people on earth, and according to some projections we will be more than nine billion in a few decades. However, if we are concerned about overpopulating our earth, we should be more concerned about the number of farm animals we bring into existence, since the number of farm animals we have on earth easily dwarfs the number of humans. We kill more than 50 billion animals every year in order to eat them, and that is just land animals alone, and we spend many of our resources on these – we for instance feed them with nearly 40 percent of all the grain in the world, which is more than enough grain to feed another two billion people.[48]

Livestock is also polluting the environment in ways that make many people sick. For instance, livestock farms often pollute the environment with ammonia that comes from decaying manure, and getting ammonia in our lungs can be dangerous:

Breathing high concentrations of ammonia can cause fluid in the lungs to build up and possible lung damage. Exposure to high levels of ammonia can burn the eyes, skin, throat, and lungs. Breathing lower concentrations of ammonia can cause coughing, wheezing, shortness of breath, laryngitis, headaches, fever, nausea, vomiting, pink frothy phlegm, chest pain, asthma, rapid pulse, and increased blood pressure.[49]

And ammonia pollution is no small nor cheap problem; as a recent study found: "[...] ammonia pollution linked to U.S. farming may impose human health costs that are greater than the profits earned by agricultural exports."[50] Speaking of manure, the amount of solid animal waste produced every year in the United States alone is estimated to be more than 130 billion tons, which is more than 80 times greater than the amount of waste from all humans in the United States, where one person averagely produces 5 tons of solid waste each year.[51] This huge amount of waste from animals also has consequences for human health, for instance when it comes to the nitrate-contamination that manure causes:

The EPA found that nitrates are the most widespread agricultural contaminant in drinking water wells and estimates that 4.5 million people are exposed to elevated nitrate levels from drinking water wells. Nitrates, if they find their way into the groundwater, can potentially be fatal to infants.[52]

So, as we have seen, both in terms of the

energy, land and water we use, meat is a very ineffective and wasteful way to feed humans. It produces enormous amounts of waste, and it causes pollution of both our air and water that is harmful for our health. It seems clear that if we are concerned about overpopulation, waste pollution, limited resources and the environment in general[53] – or again, if we just care about human health and human lives, which the pollution from livestock also puts at risk – then we should stop eating animals and anything from them.

Another way in which our practice of raising and eating animals is bad for human beings is that it is a force of global inequality and hunger in poor nations. In the United States and Europe we feed our farm animals with crops like soy and grain that are grown and transported from South America and Africa. So in many nations that are plagued by hunger, food is being exported to animal farmers who are able to give more money for it than the people who live in those nations. In this way, the industry that provides meat and our buying of this meat is causing hunger in developing countries. As the philosopher David Pearce has noted, Ethiopia is a disastrous example of this:

> Over the past few decades, millions of Ethiopians have died of "food shortages" while Ethiopia grew grain to sell to the West to feed cattle. Western meat-eating habits prop up the price of grain so that poor people in the developing world can't afford to buy it. In consequence, they starve by the millions.[54]

It is clear at this point that going vegan would be better for humanity, and even that our not being vegan is indefensible – both to ourselves and to our fellow human beings, since our farming and eating animals inevitably causes needless human misery and death. It pollutes the environment in ways that make people sick, it contributes to hunger in developing countries, it is a catalyst for making our otherwise life-saving antibiotics ineffective, and it causes lethal diseases to spread to, and kill, human beings. We do not need to eat animals or anything from them in order to be healthy – there is no fundamental need for it, and there is therefore no strong case for farming and eating animals, while all of the points mentioned above make a strong case against it. The arguments in favor of doing it are basically that certain animal parts and things from them taste good and that eating them is an old tradition, but these are not good reasons to keep on doing it, since taste and tradition obviously should not be prioritized higher than human lives and human health. So there is clearly nothing misanthropic about going vegan – quite the opposite, since going vegan clearly would be better for humanity.

THE ANIMALS WE EAT

So far we have only looked at human beings, and seen that if we only care about human beings, we have a clear obligation to go vegan since our farming and eating animals causes needless human misery and death. As we all know, however, human beings are not the only beings involved in relation to whether we should go vegan or not, since the animals we bring into existence in order for them to provide meat, dairy or eggs are relevant to consider too. So let us now include the lives of the animals we farm and/or kill in our consideration over whether we should be eating animals and things from them or not.

It is estimated that more than 99 percent of all

the billions of animals raised and slaughtered in the United States come from factory farms.[55] This percentage may be lower in other countries, but it is very likely still the vast majority of the land animals we eat in the West who live their lives on factory farms. This is clearly ethically problematic, because it cannot be doubted that factory farming makes animals suffer enormously, and that this suffering is unnecessary, because again, we do not need anything from animals in order to be healthy. There is no good or necessary reason to make animals suffer in this way from a human perspective, and, needless to say, neither is there a good reason to make animals suffer from the perspective of the animals themselves. Most people seem to agree that the animal suffering that factory farming causes is not defensible, and that it is even condemnable. So in spite of the fact that we throw our money after this industry that needlessly makes animals suffer, we agree, at least in our convictions, about the basic principle that we cannot justify making animals suffer needlessly – we seem to agree that we cannot defend buying the vast majority of the meat we buy, and that we should not support this industry. However, many people still seem to think that eating animals can be justifiable if only the animals live good lives and are killed painlessly (which still leaves open the mystery as to why most of us are in fact supporting an industry that obviously does make animals suffer immensely). It is wort taking a closer look at this "happy" meat position.

It has already been established that we do not need to eat animals in order to be healthy, so the natural question that arises is: what could justify that we kill an animal who is living a good life, or just any sentient being, in order to eat it? The answers we give to this question are that we like the taste of animal flesh and that it is convenient to eat it. These answers are problematic because they are obviously in conflict with another ethical principle that practically all of us agree upon, namely that we cannot justify killing another sentient being unless there is a necessary reason for doing so. And we must admit that neither convenience nor our liking the taste of meat comprise anything close to what could reasonably be called a necessary reason for killing a sentient being. This stands crystal clear for us when it comes to sentient beings whose sentience we have really connected with and acknowledged. For instance, we find it absurd to suggest that it would be okay to painlessly kill a pet or a human being in order to make "tasty" dinners, irrespective of whether we have treated the pet or the human well or not. We recognize that the taste of pet or human clearly cannot justify the kill. We are unfortunately slow to acknowledge the same thing when it comes to the animals we eat, seemingly because we have not truly connected with the fact of their sentience, and this failure to connect makes us keep these animals outside of our sphere of moral consideration.

To a great extend, we seem to objectify the animals we eat. Unlike our fellow humans and our pets, we seem to perceive the animals we eat partly as things rather than unequivocally seeing them as sentient beings. We see them as an 'it' rather than a 'him' or a 'her'. We need to wake up from this view, because it is unjustifiable. The beings we eat are just as able to feel and worthy of moral consideration as our pets whom we love and protect, and we should, as we do when it comes to our pets, view the animals we currently eat, along with all other sentient animals, as ends in themselves. This view, which most of us probably agree we should have – the view that sentient animals should be considered to be ends in themselves and not merely means to an end – obviously obliges us to not support the raising and killing of them for unnecessary and trivial purposes such as taste, since that clearly is to ultimately treat animals as nothing but means to an end.

That the killing of animals for mere pleasure is not justifiable – that it is in fact morally reprehensible – is easy to see when we ex-change the pleasure of taste with sadistic pleasure. Most of us condemn people who kill animals because they take pleasure in seeing the animals die for the obvious reason that this bizarre pleasure does not justify taking the life of an animal. However, when we condemn these people – when we point our morally judging fingers at someone who is shooting animals for a good laugh or cuts their throats for a rush from seeing blood – we completely overlook that killing an animal for the pleasure of taste actually is no more necessary than killing for sadistic pleasure, and therefore no more justified. It seems that we have an intuitive idea that killing an animal in order to eat it is somehow a noble thing to do – a noble and necessary evil in some way – but this idea is wrong in this day and age, and our belief that there is a relevant distinction between killing an animal for fun and killing an animal in order to eat it in today's modern society is simply a moral illusion – a very widespread one for sure.

As has been made clear, we do not need to eat animals or anything from them in order to be healthy, and it is about time we realize this fact and its implications: that we cannot justify killing animals in order to eat them, because until we do, we will keep on acting in ways that in the most relevant regards are practically indistinguishable from the evil actions of a sadistic animal killer, although on a scale that by far exceeds what even the most vicious sadist could keep up with in his wildest dreams, as we needlessly kill about 2000 land animals every second, and far more marine animals, in order for them to be eaten. Summed up shortly: If we buy meat, no matter how "happy" that meat is, we are inevitably supporting something that we all actively condemn: the needless killing of a sentient being – killing for mere pleasure.

Many attempts have been made to justify our practice of killing and eating certain animals and to downplay the horror of this practice. One of them is the argument that we humans have traits that other animals do not possess, for instance a sophisticated ability to plan for the future and an ability to communicate verbally, and since other animals lack these abilities, we are justified in killing them in order to eat them. Pointing toward distinguishing cognitive traits and depth as something that justifies our killing of sentient animals is a strange move for various reasons. First of all, no matter how much more one values human life over the life of other animals, we still have no need to eat animals, and killing animals in order to eat them is therefore still unjustified, as there is no trade-off between fundamental needs of humans and other animals in the first place – and, as pointed out in the previous chapter, if human life and health is what we value, we should actually abolish raising, killing and eating animals. Secondly, the argument is strange because it breaks down the moment we apply it to a human being who lacks certain cognitive traits. For instance, no civilized person would suggest that it would be justifiable to kill a multi-handicapped human being for the reason that he or she has no ability to speak or plan for the future. Such a suggestion is absurd and morally reprehensible, exactly because the notion that a being's lack of certain cognitive traits should make it justifiable to kill this being when there is no need to is absurd and morally reprehensible.

Another common defense of our practice of farming and killing animals is that these animals would not exist if we did not bring them into existence to be slaughtered and eaten, and therefore their lives are what makes it justifiable that we farm, kill and eat them. Again, this is a very strange argument, as it can seem to suggest that we humans have taken on a noble burden by raising, killing and eating animals – that we do it for their sake. Nothing could be further from the truth. If we really cared deeply about the animals we eat, and if we really brought them into existence for their own sake, we would not kill and eat them, since we obviously do not kill and eat those we really care about. It is of course true that the animals we have on our farms would not exist if we had not brought them into existence, but this fact in itself in no way suggests that our bringing them into existence is in fact justified.

But could it not be the case that we actually are doing something ethically praiseworthy when we bring animals into existence in order to eat them? In short: No. The reality is that we are causing immense suffering by bringing animals into existence in order to eat them. There is little doubt that it would have been better for the vast majority of the animals we keep in our farms today if we had not brought them into existence, which is to say that the vast majority of animals we keep in our farms live lives that are not worth living, but worth being spared from. This may again sound like a bombastic claim, but please consider what it is like to live a life where your mother is killed while you are young, a life where you are confined to live on little space while you are fed with food that makes you grow at an unnatural rate – often resulting in horrible joint pains – and a life where you are taken away to be slaughtered shortly after you have brought little younglings of your own into the world who will now suffer the same life. This is the reality of the lives of the vast majority of the animals we eat, and such a life does seem, rather clearly in fact, to be a life that is not worth living but worth being spared from – a life of suffering on a factory of perpetual suffering.

That the notion that we are justified in killing animals in order to eat them because we have brought them into existence is wrong and anything but an expression of moral wisdom becomes obvious when we exchange the all too abstract idea of "animals" we employ here for beings whom we actually do fully acknowledge as sentient beings who are ends in themselves, such as human beings. We do not accept the notion that parents are justified in killing their own child because they brought the child into existence, which just shows that this notion is not a valid one: that bringing a being into

existence obviously is not a sufficient justification for killing that being or treating it badly
in any way.

If we insist on bringing domesticated animals
into existence when there is no fundamental
need to, and it is a separate discussion whether
we even should do that in the first place, then
we should at least apply a basic maxim that we
all recognize applies when it comes to bringing
children into existence: we should not bring
beings into existence unless we can provide
good lives for them – and we should obviously
not kill them. To not be able to live up to this
maxim is to irresponsibly bring life into this
world, and that is exactly what we are doing in
the case of the vast majority of animals we
bring into existence.

Another very common argument for killing
animals for their flesh is that it is natural to do
so, or that it is an old tradition. This argument is
common in many ethical discussions, and it is
equally invalid in all of them for the obvious
reason that there is not necessarily anything

good about that which we deem natural or traditional. To equate "natural" and "traditional" with "good" or "ethically justified" is a mistake, and this is easy to see when we consider other "natural" and "traditional" aspects of life. Rape and murder are for instance "natural" and "traditional" in the sense that they have been universally present in all human societies, but this obviously does not suggest that these "noble traditions" are actually good. Indeed, it is obvious that they are not, which makes it obvious that the "but it is natural/traditional" is not an ethical argument, but, at best, an ambiguous statement of an irrelevant fact.

Lastly, there is the objection that we do not know, and cannot know, which life forms have the capacity to feel a continuum of joy and suffering, and therefore we cannot know what is ethical to eat and what is not. The premise of this objection is simply not true, since we clearly can make inferences about which beings have such capacities by identifying the physical states that correlate with them, and these inferences need not be more ambiguous than our inference that other people have these capacities. So we *can* make very qualified estimates about which life forms can suffer by looking at their traits, and we should always base our decisions on these – on our best estimates about what is the case. So which life forms can we be reasonably sure are sentient beings with a capacity to feel a continuum of more or less pleasant experiences? It seems safe to at least include all vertebrates, and very likely also cephalopods, given the fact that a capacity to feel suffering seems to depend on very deep and "old" structures in the nervous system that are found in some form in all vertebrates, which includes all fish, amphibians, reptiles, birds and mammals, and analogs to these structures also seem to exist in at least some cephalopods, such as octopuses.[56] So the question we must ask ourselves is: Why take the life of any such being whom we can be reasonably sure is sentient and has a capacity to feel pain and pleasure in some form when we do not need to? Indeed, why take the life of any being whom we can just reasonably suspect is conscious if we have absolutely no need to?

Our earlier-mentioned tendency to view the animals we eat more like objects than like sentient beings is not so difficult to understand when we look at the culture we find ourselves in. After all, this view is exactly the view that our culture reflects and what we have grown up with: we see the animals we eat as objects on our plate, and we thereby learn to conceive of their flesh as food – as part of our dinner rather than as a part from what was once a sentient being who had to die in order to be on our plate. What we do continually shapes how our minds perceive the world, and when we keep on eating animals, we keep on confirming and reinforcing our view of animals as food instead of as sentient beings. There is clearly a conflict between seeing something as food and seeing something, or rather some*one*, as a sentient being who deserves moral consideration, and it will therefore be hard to connect with the fact that we are eating the flesh of what was once a sentient being as long as we eat animals and view them as food. This is why we should stop eating animal flesh irrespective of its origin: because the act of eating animals sustains and reinforces our view of animals as food instead of as sentient beings, which makes ethical clear-sight elude us when it comes to the animals we eat.

This may strike many people as an out-rageous point of little moral relevance – "So now we should not eat animals because it affects our mere *view* of them?" – but this is really because we are blind to the work that our "mere view" really does in the world: it is what guides our actions and our notions of right and wrong. Our "mere view" of animals as food is what prevents us from really viewing them as sentient beings who have moral value, and it is in this way that eating them has terrible consequences. Again, this is not hard to see when we change our focus to beings we do care about: pets and people. If we began to eat pets and people, and if we began to consider this a normal practice, it would inevitably be a degradation of our view of these as sentient beings and pull us closer in the direction of viewing them as objects, and such a view has consequences – horrible consequences. It was for instance exactly the object-conception of individuals of certain races – the view of certain people as instruments rather than ends – that kept these people as slaves in certain cultures in the past, and kept the slaveholders and society at large from seeing anything really wrong about it; and in times of war, this conception of certain groups of people as being mere things rather than sentient beings has effectively strangled compassion toward them, innumerable times unfortunately, and paved the way for incomprehensible genocides. We have unfortunately learned little from history, because the same unquestioned and unchallenged objectifying view and complete lack of compassion toward sentient beings still thrives today: it is the view we have and keep on reinforcing in relation to the animals we are eating, and, as a result, we are committing a holocaust for the sake of mere pleasure.

As long as people kept having slaves and kept promulgating the view that certain people were work instruments rather than sentient ends in themselves, basic ethical sanity eluded them, and slavery persisted. Likewise, as long as we keep on eating animals – as long as we see them as food rather than seeing them, unequivocally, as sentient beings who are ends in themselves – we will not be able to view them as we should, and we will keep on being numb to their suffering and keep on treating them as the objects we perceive them to be rather than as the sentient ends they are.

So we should stop eating any meat from animals so that we can finally begin to transcend our view of certain animals as mere things to be eaten – the view that causes us to be practically indifferent to the atrocities that are being committed against them. Once we abandon this view there will be no point of return, and we will finally be able to see just how unethical our view of animals has been; our finding it okay to kill them for the sake of palate pleasure for instance – a view that will un-doubtedly embarrass ourselves and our descen-dants in the future.

Another problem with "happy meat" is that it is even less sustainable to raise "happy meat" and that these "happy" free ranging animals are at greater risk of many diseases than animals who are confined inside in stinky halls. It has for instance been found that grass-fed animals emit significantly higher amounts of greenhouse gases than animals who are "factory farmed":

Since grazing animals eat mostly cellulose-rich roughage while their feedlot counter-parts eat mostly simple sugars whose digestion requires no rumination, the grazing animals emit two to four times as much methane, a greenhouse gas roughly

30 times more powerful than carbon dioxide.[57]

So the more animals we farm on grass instead of inside stinky factory farm halls – a step of regulation that many people seem to advocate as the step we should take when presented with the realities of factory farming – the greater will we make the already enormous impact of animal agriculture on the environment.

Secondly, as mentioned, so-called free-ranging animals are exposed to greater risks of various diseases such as parasitic infections. For instance, the parasite *Toxoplasma gondii*, which is the cause of the disease toxoplasmosis, had reportedly been practically eliminated, but it has again become more prevalent as organically raised pigs have become fashionable again, and this is not surprising since "pigs raised in outdoor systems inherently confront higher risks of exposure to foodborne parasites, particularly T. gondii."[58] Furthermore, free-range eggs have been found to have higher concentrations of highly toxic dioxins than non-free-range, and meat from free-range pigs has been found to be more contaminated with E. coli.[59]

So, at least in these ways, it would actually be worse for humanity – we would be exposed to greater risks of certain diseases and cause greater methane emissions – if we "evolved" to only farm "happy meat" compared to what we are doing now. This obviously does not make a case for factory farming, but instead destroys the notion that anything short of abolishing animal farming is going to solve the environmental and health-related problems it causes. We should not "evolve" beyond factory farming to free-range, but evolve beyond killing animals for their flesh entirely, and even some free-range animal farmers have come out of the closet and admitted this. One of these is pig farmer Bob Comis who raises free-range pigs "humanely." In a recent article called *The Importance of Our Evolution Beyond Killing for Food* he admits that no matter how well we treat animals, killing them in order to eat them is wrong:

> What I do is wrong, in spite of its acceptance by nearly 95 percent of the American population. I know it in my bones -- even if I cannot yet act on it. Someday it must stop. Somehow we need to become the sort of beings who can see what we are doing when we look head on, the sort of beings who don't weave dark, damning shrouds to sustain, with acceptance and celebration, the grossly unethical. Deeper, much deeper, we have an obligation to eat otherwise.
> It might take incalculable generations of being hooked by and grappling with the ethics of slaughter to get there. But we really do need to get there -- because again, what I am doing, what we are doing, is wrong, even terribly so.[60]

There is of course a profound dissonance bet- ween this farmer's convictions and his actions, but he is not much different from the rest of us in this regard, as the same dissonance is found in ourselves when we say that we find it wrong to kill a sentient being for mere pleasure, and yet buy meat and thereby support an industry that does exactly that. Just like this farmer, we somehow manage to completely fail to act in accordance with our deepest convictions and core values.

It is an unfortunate irony that the notion that it in principle is okay to raise and kill animals in order to eat them as long as we treat them well and kill them painlessly is a notion that in practice causes us to inflict extreme amounts of suffering upon animals. But it is actually not so hard to explain why this is so – why this "in principle" argument that seems to be against suffering ends up causing so much suffering – because, in practice, that is all it possibly ever could. As is evident in our practices guided by this principle today, it is the first step on a slippery slope that inevitably leads to practices that cause enormous amounts of suffering for animals. This is inevitable because the "in principle" argument implicitly rests on the idea that animals ultimately are commodities – instruments for use rather than ends in themselves. And again, when we have that view of other beings – when beings fall more in the "objects" category in our minds than in the "sentient beings" category – our ethically relevant emotions toward them are effectively turned off; we fail to empathize and connect with their sentience, and we effectively begin to treat them as objects. That is exactly what we do today: raise and treat animals as objects, kill them as objects, cut them into parts, put these parts in packages, distribute the parts to stores, buy the parts in the stores as objects, cook them and eat them as objects. What the "in principle" argument inevitably results in in practice is that animals become property and things to be treated for the profits of those who own, kill and sell them, and in this quest for profit, the concern for animals simply ends up losing in practice, as witnessed by the animal farm practices we see today – including the so-called "humane" ones, as documented here: http://www.peacefulprairie.org/humane-myth.html.[61]

So the fact is that the "in principle" argument inevitably leads to anything but "treating animals well" in practice, and this is another reason why it should be rejected; and of course also for the reason that treating a being well cannot possibly involve needlessly killing that being – something we can again easily see if we substitute "animals" for beings we do have moral concern for and do perceive as ends in themselves – which just reveals that, if we really take it seriously, the "in principle" argument is self-refuting: treating someone well cannot be reconciled with needlessly killing him or her.

So the final conclusion is that we cannot defend raising and killing animals in order to eat them from the perspective of the animals either. We cannot, neither in principle nor in practice, defend killing a sentient being for mere pleasure, which is exactly what we do when we farm and kill animals in order to eat them. We clearly have an obligation to the animals to stop the needless killing of them, and to stop eating them altogether, since eating them only reinforces our view of them as objects, which clearly is in conflict with unequivocally viewing them as sentient beings who are ends in themselves, and this objectifying view evidently causes us to treat the animals as objects, and to make them suffer immensely.

WHY NOT JUST BE VEGETARIAN?

So we cannot defend needlessly killing animals or defend eating them at all. "But", one may ask, "why not just be vegetarian, then? Why should we not eat eggs or dairy?" The short answer: Because it also causes immense amounts of suffering. In many ways.

First of all there are the reasons directly related to human life and health that were reviewed in previous chapters: intake of eggs is strongly linked to increased all-cause mortality risk[62] and diabetes,[63] dairy intake is linked to breast and prostate cancer,[64] and raising billions of egg-laying hens and millions of milk-providing cows significantly increases the risk of zoonotic diseases, including mass killing pandemics, which may be one of the dangers that are most likely to pose a so-called existential risk.

So compelling reasons to stop farming animals and to stop consuming dairy and eggs for the sake of human beings have already been presented, and it has been pointed out that we even have an obligation to our fellow human beings to help stop farming animals. Yet this is far from the full story since the "production" of dairy and eggs obviously also involves animals, and we also have an obligation to them to stop exploiting them. When we look at the reality of the egg and dairy industry, or when we just think about what eating dairy and eggs actually amounts to, it becomes obvious that the idea that it is somehow virtuous and respectful to animals to be vegetarian – to "merely" consume eggs and dairy – hardly could be more wrong.

First of all, it is a common misconception that dairy and egg "production" does not involve killing any animals. All dairy cows and egg-laying chickens end up hanging upside down in a slaughterhouse alongside the cows and chickens who were raised for their flesh, and by buying eggs and dairy one does inevitably support this end too: the needless death of the animal who had her eggs or milk taken from her. This is not the only death in the egg and dairy industry, however. In both the dairy and egg industry, males are useless – they are trash, and as a result, they are treated exactly as such. Male chicks are killed shortly after they have hatched, a process that is euphemistically referred to as 'chick culling', which usually either happens by throwing them into a grinding machine while alive (not for the faint-hearted: http://www.youtube.com/watch?v=JJ—faib7to), by breaking their necks or by suffocating them with gas. These practices of killing male chicks are standard in the entire egg industry – including the part of it that provides eggs that are labeled "free-range", "organic" and "humane." Similarly, in the dairy industry, newborn male calves will never give milk, and they are therefore taken away from their mothers shortly after they are born, killed as young calves, cut into parts, put on packages and sold as veal. Again, this is the standard procedure no matter the labeling. So nothing could be more wrong than to claim that our eating eggs and dairy does not involve death.

Death is not the only sad and horrible aspect of the egg and dairy industry, however, because so is life itself for the animals. Egg-laying hens are not magic egg-laying machines, and they are therefore commonly, whether "free-range" or not, force molted – that is, completely starved in up to two weeks which provokes them into a new laying cycle – and they are then killed after about 18 months when they are considered worn out.[65] A short and brutish life indeed. Similarly, cows are not magic milk-providers; they, like humans and most other mammals, must have been pregnant in order to lactate. For this reason, cows are made pregnant throughout their entire lives, usually through insemination, which involves "[...] a person inserting his arm far into the cow's rectum in order to position the uterus, and then forcing an instrument into her vagina."[66] This is the life of the dairy cow: a perpetual cycle of painful insemination, pregnancy, and then giving birth to her calve who is taken away from her shortly after. So not only do the industries of eggs and dairy involve an extreme amount of death, they also involve lives that are full of unimaginable, yet completely unnecessary, pain and suffering.

It is not merely buying eggs and dairy that we should abstain from, however – we should also stop consuming it. Just like we should abstain from eating meat because it reinforces a morally defunct view of animals, so too should we abstain from eating eggs and dairy. In a subtle but powerful way, eating eggs and dairy is still to support the industry that provides these, because it inevitably sends the signal that milk and eggs are morally unproblematic to buy and consume, which they surely are not. Secondly, and much more generally, eating eggs and dairy also promotes and reinforces a more fundamental view that has broader implications, which is the view that chickens and cows – and animals in general – are beings, or rather resources, whom we can take from and exploit for our mere pleasure. We need to stop reinforcing this view, because again, what this view basically does is that it makes us morally numb to the animals we currently exploit – blind and indifferent to their suffering, so indifferent that we cannot be moved to act even when we see the greatest of atrocities committed against them, such as mass killings of newly hatched chicks. It all comes back to our flawed view of animals – the cold and apathetic view we presently have of the animals we exploit, which inevitably causes us to inflict immense amounts of suffering upon them. It is about time we stop reinforcing that view. It is about time we transcend it completely.

CONCLUSION

It should be clear at this point that we should go vegan. We are using our resources to export food from countries where human beings die of starvation, and this we do in order to feed animals who live terrible lives, and we then kill these animals and eat their meat in amounts that raises our mortality risk significantly. Furthermore, our raising of animals pollutes the environment massively in various ways – it for instance pollutes our air and water in ways that make us sick – and it increases the risk of the spread of lethal diseases and causes thousands, if not millions, of human deaths every year. When we keep in mind the fact that we do this completely unnecessarily – as we have no need to eat anything from animals in order to be healthy – what we are doing seems nothing less than masochistic.

There are so many good reasons to stop our practice of animal farming, many of them are alone sufficient to make a clear case that we should indeed do this, and together they make the case overwhelmingly clear. We are perpetuating and supporting something that is bad for every being who is involved in it, with the possible exception of those who make money from animal farming. So why do most of us still support this unnecessary practice of animal farming when it has so bad consequences and causes so much suffering? As mentioned, we do it partly out of habit and tradition – it is what we are used to, and what our culture has taught us is normal, acceptable and perhaps even normative. Secondly, we do it because we are not well-informed about the relevant facts about the system we are supporting and its consequences. Most people seem unaware of the fact that we do not need anything from animals in order to be healthy;

we seem unaware of the fact that our unnecessary practice of farming animals costs thousands of human lives every year; we seem unaware of the waste, pollution and inefficiency of animal farming; we seem unaware of the consequences that modern animal farming has for developing countries; we seem unaware of the suffering that the animals we eat undergo during their lives, and we even seem to fail to realize the obvious fact that a sentient animal had to be killed – still unnecessarily – in order for its flesh to be on our plate. These facts are generally well-hidden from us, and that is how something that in every way goes against the core values we all share can keep on existing – by virtue of our ignorance basically. As is almost always the case, ignorance about what we are doing is very costly.

Fortunately, since it is only due to tradition and ignorance that we continue our harmful practice of eating animals and things from them, the remedy is quite simple and obvious: to challenge the tradition and spread the relevant facts – to educate people and help them act according to their own values. Because if one simply shares the value that we should avoid unnecessary suffering and death – a value that most of us hold for sure – then one also agrees that we should stop farming and exploiting animals and instead go vegan, which is clear in light of the consequences that animal farming has, and also obvious from what it intrinsically *is* in this day and age: a practice of needlessly killing and exploiting animals. So what is needed is that we spread the relevant facts about what we are doing so that people can act according to their own values. This educational mission of spreading this information stands as our ethical obligation, and it is clearly the royal road toward a better world.

This spread of information is already taking place, and a transition seems to gradually be on the way. Given the spread of information and the raising of awareness that the Internet makes possible, the moral progress that our species seems to have undergone continually through-out its history, and the new vegan products and technologies that seem to be emerging at an exponential rate (it will, for instance, soon be possible to make foods that are completely similar to meat, eggs and dairy in terms of taste and texture which involve absolutely no animals in the production process, and since these foods will not involve the expensive and wasteful "steps" of raising and killing animals, these foods can and will eventually be very cheap, and thereby outcompete the more expensive dairy, eggs and animal body parts), I consider it likely that the majority of the Western population will be vegan within 15 years, and from then on it will not take long before we reach 100 percent. In fact, only a small percentage of the population, maybe ten percent or even less, will need to make this transition and speak out about its urgency in order to get the snowball rolling, because it will only require small cracks in the foundation of social acceptance that holds the practice of animal farming in place in order to bring this practice into question and gradually make it socially *un*acceptable. And once that happens, we will be at a point of no return, and we will see the world go vegan permanently. I think this transition is unavoidable and that it will happen very soon, but we must still do whatever we can to make it happen as fast and soon as possible in order to minimize the unnecessary suffering and death that our practice of animal farming causes.

So it is up to us now. We can end all this suffering. We simply need to realize that we have a choice – realize that there is an easily available alternative to our practice of raising, killing and eating animals – and then make the choice that is in alignment with our own core values: to stop any support of animal farming and to stop eating anything from animals at all. Because as long as the demand persists, and as long as we reinforce the view that killing and exploiting animals unnecessarily is okay, the misery imposing industry of animal farming will persist. The enormous amount of suffering it causes – both for humans and other animals – will persist. We can stop this entirely by not demanding or buying anything from animals and by fundamentally changing our view. And we must go forward and do this – we are obliged to ourselves, our descendants and our fellow sentient beings to do this.

So why should we go vegan? Because, as we have seen, there are so many good reasons to go vegan, while there are not really any good reasons not to. Because it is the only rational and ethically defensible thing to do. Because it is a big step in the direction away from enormous amounts of unnecessary suffering and toward a more intelligent and more flourishing world. That is why we should go vegan.

RECOMMENDED RESOURCES

I find the following to be particularly good sources of information on nutrition:

Michael Greger, M.D:

http://nutritionfacts.org/

Jack Norris, R.D:

http://www.veganhealth.org/

A movie that seems to have inspired many people to see more clearly on this subject is the full length movie *Earthlings* that can be watched here (contains disturbing images):

http://earthlings.com/?page_id=32

The following short clip also seems to have made an impression on many people. It seems especially effective for the purpose of helping people to connect with the fact that a sentient being has to die in order for there to be meat on our plate (contains no bloody images):
http://www.youtube.com/watch?v=LUkHkyy4uqw#t=3

I also find the book *The Hedonistic Imperative* by David Pearce to be highly recommendable. It is free and available online at:
http://www.hedweb.com/hedab.htm.

PDF download:

https://cl.nfshost.com/david-pearce-the-hedonistic-imperative.pdf

APPENDIX – REFUTATION OF REMAINING COMMON OBJECTIONS

But some people can't survive unless they eat meat.

Whether some people need to eat meat in order to survive or not changes nothing for all of us who do not need to eat meat or anything else that comes from animals in order to be healthy. The conclusion stands unchanged: Those of us who can go vegan – that is, everyone living in a modern society – clearly should.

But you will kill animals no matter what. Plant agriculture inevitably kills animals too.

It is true that animals unfortunately are killed in plant agriculture, for instance when we harvest, but that does not justify needlessly killing billions of animals more in order to eat them. Secondly, the fact that plant agriculture costs animal lives only makes a stronger case that we should stop farming animals, because the more animals we farm, the more crops we will need to grow in order to feed these farmed animals compared to if we fed our crops directly to human beings, and animal agriculture therefore just increases the number of animals killed in plant agriculture.

People should eat what they want to eat.
We probably all agree with the notion that we should all be allowed to do whatever we want as long as we do not harm other beings in the process, and that is probably also what lies behind the sentiment expressed above. The problem, however, is that eating animals and things from animals clearly *does* harm other beings, including humans when we look at it in the bigger picture. We unfortunately miss this fact because the harm that animal agriculture

causes, both to humans and to animals, is anything but transparent: we hide the fact that animals are being killed needlessly, and we do not see the harmful consequences of animal farming because it is so big and complex a system. So in short: People should not just eat what they want to eat when their eating habits cause needless suffering and death, as many of our eating habits do.

What about getting enough calcium, which we usually get from milk, and enough iron and vitamin D, which we usually get from meat?

Fortunately, we do not need to consume dairy to get calcium, and we do not need to eat animal parts in order to get iron and vitamin D. Both calcium and iron can be found in plenty amounts in fruits and vegetables. Kale, Broccoli, cabbage, celery, garlic and oranges for instance all contain lots of calcium – in fact, many of these contain considerably higher concentrations of calcium than cows milk, while foods such as nuts, legumes and kale easily can provide sufficient amounts of iron. Vitamin D can easily be obtained through exposure to sunlight, and if one cannot get enough sunlight, a vegan vitamin D supplement is an obvious solution.

Vegan foods are not so tasty, and I don't know how to make vegan food either.

This is merely an expression of a lack of experience. Vegan foods can be extremely tasty, and making vegan food is not hard. If you don't know how to make delicious vegan food, it is probably because you have never attempted to make delicious vegan food. So to go ahead and try would be a good first step – and it can both be easy and very delicious.

We become detached from nature if we stop farming animals.

This claim is absurd. Why should it follow that we become detached from nature if we stop farming animals? It doesn't. We can enjoy nature just the same after we stop farming animals as we can now, and in some cases even better, since it in many places will mean that one can finally take a deep breath of fresh air when one walks outside instead of inhaling harmful and sharply smelling ammonia which currently pollutes our air in large areas of otherwise idyllic wild nature.

What about plants? Are they not living beings?

Plants are surely living organisms in the biological sense of the word, but we have no more reason to suspect that plants are sentient beings who can feel a continuum of pleasant and unpleasant experiences than we have reason to suspect that a rock can have such experiences. They simply have none of the features that we find give rise to this.

But we need animals for our soil.

First of all, various vegan farm practices currently in action prove that we can farm without exploiting animals. Secondly, even if domesticated animals were necessary for the health of our soil, that would in no way imply that we would need to slaughter and eat them.

Once we have artificially grown meat, then we will have an obligation to stop eating animals, but not before.
This is simply wrong. The ethical status of eating animals is exactly the same today as it will be when so-called in vitro meat is available: we do not need to eat it. If one wants to point toward a technological breakthrough that clearly makes eating things from animals indefensible it is one that already has happened: the mass production of vitamin B12 from non-animal sources.

I once ate a plant-based diet, but I began feeling protein deficiency, so I began eating meat again, and I suddenly felt better. I cannot justify eating meat, but given my experience with not eating it, I do it anyway.

How does protein deficiency feel compared to, say, vitamin B12 deficiency? If you are deficient in something, you cannot feel what it is you are deficient in, no matter how good you are at observing your inner state. You have to get a blood test. I would say that protein deficiency sounds very unlikely since it is quite hard to eat in a way that would lead to protein deficiency. Vitamin B12 deficiency sounds far more likely if you did not supplement your diet with it. But again, you should consult your doctor in order to find our what the cause of your problem is, and not rely on introspection on this one. Again, we can have optimal health on a vegan diet, and, as should be clear from what has been presented in this book, mere laziness is not a valid reason for not going vegan; everything we can get from eating meat, eggs or dairy that might be good for us can be obtained from vegan sources today, and to not choose these vegan sources over animal sources is just laziness.

But my actions change virtually nothing. Animal farming and exploitation will still persist, and there will just be one person less who consumes meat, eggs and dairy.

If we all adopt that view, then we surely will not see any change. However, you *do* make a difference by changing your actions, not only in the way that you no longer support this industry financially, but also when you just tell people that you are vegan. When you do this, you first of all help gradually make it socially acceptable and more normal to be vegan, and you make people realize that we do not need to eat anything from animals in order to be healthy, and that living on a vegan diet is not difficult. You also make people think about their own choices, cause them to ask questions, and ignite conversations that enlighten, challenge and expand people's views. People are often more open to change than we think. It should be remembered that in the ocean of our shared world view and culture, small ripples *can* cause enormous waves, and together our small ripples can create constructive interference for the better in our culture.

Other animals eat us and each other, so why should we not eat them?

This objection is based on a primitive retributive morality of a kind that makes the world blind: if others do bad things to us or each other, then we are justified in doing bad things to them. It is a rather childish notion, and one that we acknowledge to be invalid in all other aspects of life. For instance, if a child hits an adult, is the adult justified in hitting the child back? Obviously not. Yet the animals we eat stand in the same relation to us as children do, in the sense that we have brought these innocent beings into the world, and they are completely dependent on us. Secondly, the objection is fundamentally misguided since it makes a vast generalization: Because some animals do bad things, we are justified in eating all of them. The animals we eat never eat human beings, so this objection is really absurd – on many levels.

This objection is just another objection that attempts to avoid answering the simple questions that the modern omnivore is being asked: Why kill and eat a sentient being when there is no fundamental need to do so? How can we justify killing a being for mere pleasure? Pointing fingers and claiming that certain beings are not angles – something one could point one's finger in many directions and at many beings, including some humans, and exclaim – is simply not a good reason for killing them for mere palate pleasure.

What about the mosquitoes who want to eat me?

It should first of all be noted that this question also has no relevance in relation to whether we should eat meat, dairy and eggs or not. It is still indefensible to consume these no matter what unrelated and distractive question we may ask in order to slip off the hook. Secondly, basic principles of self-defense always apply, so if you think you are in danger, you are obviously justified to take appropriate action in order to avoid harm. However, it is generally a good idea to avoid ending up in the alley with mosquitoes in the first place, as they tend to get you in the end. So the best advice here, as is always the case when it comes to self-defense, is to try to avoid any danger in the first place.

It is okay to be a vegan if you are active on a normal level, but you just cannot be a fit athlete, especially not an explosive bodybuilder/weightlifter-type, on a purely plant-based diet.

This is simply false, and one can point to numerous examples of people who debunk that myth. For instance, Patrik Baboumian is a vegan strongman who in 2012 became European champion in raw-powerlifting and set a world record in both the disciplines fronthold and keglifting, and in 2013 he set a world record when he walked 10 meters with 550 kilograms on his shoulders. Another example is Frank Medrano whom by many is known from Youtube where he, at the time of writing, has more than ten million views on a video where he makes extreme bodyweight workout (this one: http://www.youtube.com/watch? v=RFPsvF3UOdo). As a single search on Google for "vegan athletes" reveals, successful vegan athletes can be found in virtually all disciplines ranging from weightlifting to extreme distance running. So vegans clearly can be elite athletes of all shades.

You cannot be a vegan and be intellectually active.

Once again one can easily point to some well-known people who clearly disprove that myth, for instance physicist and educator Brian Greene and molecular geneticist George M. Church who are both vegan and highly intellectually active.

I don't think killing for meat is wrong, and it is not the same as killing for fun. What makes it different is the intention behind

the kill – that is what is morally relevant.
Sure, it takes a very different person to kill an animal for fun than it takes to go down and buy some meat that one is barely aware of came from an actual sentient being – unlike people who do the former, most of the people who do the latter are compassionate people who express that they like animals. However, when we look at the system that those who buy meat collectively support and keep existing and thriving – and granted, this can be difficult since it requires that we take a step back and look at a system that is not just acting in a single moment as the sadistic killer; it acts constantly and is well-integrated and accepted in society – it becomes obvious that what this system does is actually something that, even if we just look at the intention behind, is basically not different from what the single guy who kills animals for fun does: it kills for the sake of pleasure.

Again, what accounts for the difference in our view of the sadist's actions and our own is 1) that we still in some way have the archaic belief that we need meat, 2) that the brutal realities of the industry take place out of sight behind closed doors, and 3) that eating animal parts and things from animals is part of our tradition. Our belief that we need meat is clearly false, and 2) and 3) are obviously terrible reasons, but these three sure make a strong and deceptive trio. Another fact that seems to be missing in the moral equation of those who consider killing for meat to be justified is that there really is a sentient being who has to die in order for us to eat meat – that we do not merely kill a thing – "just an animal" – but a conscious being in order to get meat. This must change – we must learn to connect with the fact of the sentience of the animals we eat, which begins by seeing them as beings, not things. As animal persons, not food.

The claim that animal farming is not justifiable and has bad consequences does not necessarily imply that we should go vegan. We could still eat animals from the wild.
In modern society, it practically does imply that,

as it is only a minority of people who can be fed by wild animals. Sure, few of us could be non-vegan without farm animals, but it would then only be few of us, and those few would then have to justify killing animals in order to eat them when they do not need to eat them – something that will be very hard in a vegan society that is neither blinded by myths about the "need" for eating animals nor by a blinding veil of tradition that causes us to denigrate the moral status of animals when it comes to eating them.

It does not follow that we should go vegan for the sake of humanity just because our current farm practices are bad for humans. We could farm in better ways that do not involve bad consequences.

It actually does follow, because we cannot provide eggs for a significant amount of the human population in any other way than by having billions of chickens lay those eggs, and billions of chickens will inevitably increase the risk of zoonotic diseases such as avian flu and SARS. A global shift to a vegan diet would remove these dangerous and unnecessary risks.

Should we not rather focus on human problems?

As is clear from the information that has been presented here, our practice of animal farming is indeed a huge human problem; it causes many problems for human beings – for example many instances of disease and death – and going vegan is the most efficient solution to many of these problems. Besides, being vegan does not in any way diminish one's ability to solve other important human problems.

A global shift to a vegan diet would cause the number of farm animals to explode, and they would then quickly overpopulate the earth.

Not so. Farm animals are brought into existence by us, often through artificial insemination, and if we stop bringing more farm animals into existence, their numbers will gradually decline.

A global shift to a vegan diet would put many farmers and companies out of business.
It sure would, and then people will have to find more benign things to do for a living. That people would lose jobs if we made this change is not a good argument for maintaining the status quo. We should prioritize the common good rather than single branches and businesses, especially when those branches are outright harmful for us.

I agree completely with the point that we should go vegan, but I just cannot stop eating both meat, eggs and dairy. I feel it would be too inconvenient and too big a personal sacrifice.
Of course you can, and it is not a sacrifice at all. As philosopher David Pearce has noted: "Giving up foods of animal origin demands no heroic personal sacrifice - merely mild personal incon-

venience." This inconvenience is mild indeed, and mild inconvenience should surely not trump the mountain of good reasons there are to go vegan – it is simply not a good reason to keep on supporting a practice that causes needless suffering and death upon human beings and other animals. Becoming vegan is not hard at all, but simply a matter of changing a habit, and of taking the right stance on an ethical issue and standing by it. Surely we can do that.

NOTES

[1] Some of these are:

Michael Greger, M.D:

http://nutritionfacts.org/

Jack Norris, R.D:

http://www.veganhealth.org/

Ginny Kisch Messina, MPH, R.D.:

http://www.theveganrd.com/

Neal Barnard, M.D:

http://www.nealbarnard.org/

Joel Fuhrman, M.D:

http://www.drfuhrman.com/

[2] Craig, Mangels & American Dietetic Association, 2009:

http://www.ncbi.nlm.nih.gov/pubmed/19562864

[3] Heart disease: Kromhout & de Goede, 2014. Link:

http://www.ncbi.nlm.nih.gov/pubmed/24345990

Brain health: Bauer et al., 2013. Link:

http://www.ncbi.nlm.nih.gov/pubmed/24285504

Aging: O'Callaghan et al., 2013. Link:
http://www.ncbi.nlm.nih.gov/pubmed/24342530

[4] Arterburn et al., 2008. Link:
http://www.ncbi.nlm.nih.gov/pubmed/18589030

[5] The following videos by Dr. Michael Greger shed some light on the risk of mercury poisoning that intake of fish seems to pose, and the case for taking vegan capsules:
http://www.youtube.com/watch?v=3l9T9t4s3uk
http://www.youtube.com/watch?v=X_RKtP4D9uI

[6] Zeilmaker et al., 2013. Link:
http://www.ncbi.nlm.nih.gov/pubmed/22079313
While some species of fish only contain mercury in amounts that are well below what is considered a safe amount, a lot seems to imply that even very small amounts of mercury have adverse effects on our brain health, and that there therefore are no safe amounts when it comes to mercury.
Another video from Michael Greger is worth watching in relation to this:
http://www.youtube.com/watch?v=dWE3UoE-18c

[7] Hoh et al., 2009. Link:
http://www.ncbi.nlm.nih.gov/pubmed/19265383
It might even be all fish oil capsules that contain PCBs since the technique currently employed to remove them seems to not remove them effectively. As Hoh et al. conclude: "This suggests that the commercial molecular distillation treatment used for removal of organic/inorganic

toxic contaminants is only effective for the lighter organic contaminants."

[8] Pan et al., 2012. Link:
http://www.ncbi.nlm.nih.gov/pubmed/22412075

[9] Ibid.

[10] Ibid.

[11] Darmadi-Blackberry et al., 2004. Link:
http://www.ncbi.nlm.nih.gov/pubmed/15228991

[12] Singh, Sabaté & Fraser, 2003. Link:
http://ajcn.nutrition.org/content/78/3/526S.long

[13] Ibid.

[14] Nachman et al., 2013. Link:
http://ehp.niehs.nih.gov/1206245/
Michael Greger has also given a good presentation on this subject:
http://www.youtube.com/watch?v=9T5IjPcaozE

[15] Silbergeld & Nachman, 2008. Link:
http://www.ncbi.nlm.nih.gov/pubmed/18991934

[16] Rohrmann et al., 2011. Link:
http://www.ncbi.nlm.nih.gov/pubmed/20473877

[17]
http://www.consumerreports.org/cro/magazine/2014/02/the
-high-cost-of-cheap-chicken/index.htm
http://trove.com/me/content/Gv4jd

[18] Ibid.

[19] Eckel, 2008. Link:
http://ajcn.nutrition.org/content/87/4/799.short

[20] Radzevičienė & Ostrauskas, 2012. Link:
http://www.ncbi.nlm.nih.gov/pubmed/22390963

[21] Melnik, 2011. Link:
http://www.ncbi.nlm.nih.gov/pubmed/21335995
Danby, 2009. Link:
http://www.ncbi.nlm.nih.gov/pmc/articles/PMC2715202/
Adebamowo et al., 2005. Link:
http://www.ncbi.nlm.nih.gov/pubmed/15692464

[22] Qin et al., 2007. Link:
http://www.ncbi.nlm.nih.gov/pubmed/17704029
Song et al., 2013. Link:
http://www.ncbi.nlm.nih.gov/pubmed/23256145
Chan et al., 2001. Link:
http://www.ncbi.nlm.nih.gov/pubmed/11566656
Kroenke et al., 2013. Link:
http://jnci.oxfordjournals.org/content/early/2013/03/08/jnci.
djt027.abstract

[23] Danby, 2009. Link:
http://www.ncbi.nlm.nih.gov/pmc/articles/PMC2715202/

[24] European Food Safety Authority, 2010. Link:
http://www.efsa.europa.eu/en/efsajournal/pub/1701.htm

[25] Günther et al., 2010. Link:

http://www.ncbi.nlm.nih.gov/pubmed/20042466

[26] McCarty, 1999. Link:
http://www.ncbi.nlm.nih.gov/pubmed/10687887

[27] Haslam & James, 2005. Link:
http://www.thelancet.com/journals/lancet/article/PIIS0140-6736(05)67483-1/fulltext
Luppino et al., 2010. Link:
http://www.ncbi.nlm.nih.gov/pubmed/20194822

[28] Tonstad et al., 2009. Link:
http://www.ncbi.nlm.nih.gov/pmc/articles/PMC2671114/

[29] Ibid.
Radzevičienė & Ostrauskas, 2012. Link:
http://www.ncbi.nlm.nih.gov/pubmed/22390963
Ellis, 2013. Link:
http://www.dailymail.co.uk/health/article-2509674/Could-eating-cheese-diabetes-Research-suggests-certain-foods-make-body-unhealthily-acidic.html

[30] Vergnaud et al., 2010. Link:
http://www.ncbi.nlm.nih.gov/pubmed/20592131

[31] Hammond & Levine, 2010. Link:
http://www.ncbi.nlm.nih.gov/pmc/articles/PMC3047996/

[32] Knutsen, 1994. Link:
http://www.ncbi.nlm.nih.gov/pubmed/8172119

[33] Orlich et al., 2013. Link:
http://www.ncbi.nlm.nih.gov/pubmed/23836264

[34] Beezhold, Johnston & Daigle, 2010. Link:
http://www.ncbi.nlm.nih.gov/pubmed/20515497

[35] Beezhold, Johnston & Daigle, 2009. Link:
https://apha.confex.com/apha/137am/webprogram/Paper2
06464.html

[36] The following video from Michael Greger provides a
very short discussion of this:
http://www.youtube.com/watch?v=mndv0JGFBMI

[37] One could of course argue, based on what we just saw
in relation to health and nutrition, that the nutritional
consequences of our practice of eating animals and things
from them by itself convincingly makes the case that we
should stop it for our own sake, and I agree that it indeed
does. However, as we shall now see, simply assuming the
nutritional consequences of our current practice to be the
same as the consequences of a practice that does not
involve raising animals, which then sets the ethical scale of
what we should do in a neutral position from this
perspective, is more than sufficient in order to convincingly
make the case that we should stop eating animals for the
sake of humanity. This assumption makes it up to the other
consequences of our practice of raising, killing and eating
animals to tip this ethical scale, and, as we shall now see,
this scale does not merely tip, but tumbles completely in
the direction that is: we should stop raising farm animals
and go vegan.

[38] Babatunde, 2011. Link:

http://www.vanguardngr.com/2011/02/livestock-diseases-africa-lacks-capacity-for-veterinary-services-reports/#sthash.RhngLYv1.dpuf

[39] Simon, 2013.

[40] Tavernise, 2013. Link:
http://www.nytimes.com/2013/09/17/health/cdc-report-finds-23000-deaths-a-year-from-antibiotic-resistant-infections.html?_r=0

[41] Bottemiller, 2011. Link:
http://www.foodsafetynews.com/2011/02/fda-confirms-80-percent-of-antibiotics-used-in-animal-ag/#.Us0tNPgvk8o
Charles, 2013. Link:
http://www.npr.org/blogs/thesalt/2013/07/11/200870193/are-antibiotics-on-the-farm-risky-business

[42] Goodland & Anhang, 2009. Link:
http://www.worldwatch.org/files/pdf/Livestock%20and%20Climate%20Change.pdf

[43] Steinfeld et al., 2006. Link:
http://www.fao.org/docrep/010/a0701e/a0701e00.htm

[44] Pimentel & Pimentel, 2003. Link:
http://ajcn.nutrition.org/content/78/3/660S.full.pdf

[45] http://www.greeneatz.com/foods-carbon-footprint.html
http://www.spiegel.de/international/germany/grossbild-574754-1283672.html

[46] Aggidis et al., 2013. Link:

http://www.imeche.org/docs/default-source/reports/Global_Food_Report.pdf?sfvrsn=0

[47] Pimentel & Pimentel, 2003. Link:
http://ajcn.nutrition.org/content/78/3/660S.full.pdf

[48] http://www.news.cornell.edu/stories/1997/08/us-could-feed-800-million-people-grain-livestock-eat
It has actually been estimated that we could feed 4 billion more people from the farm land we use today if we abandoned meat, eggs and dairy:
http://www.nbcnews.com/science/feed-4-billion-more-skip-meat-milk-eggs-study-says-6C10848930

[49]
http://toxtown.nlm.nih.gov/text_version/chemicals.php?id=2
[50] Stokstad, 2014. Link:
http://www.sciencemag.org/content/343/6168/238.summary

[51] http://www.ncifap.org/issues/environment/

[52] Ibid.

[53] Only a very few of the ways in which our eating of animals and things from them impacts the environment has been mentioned here. A more detailed – and also more dystopic – treatment of this subject can be found the books *Comfortably Unaware* and *Food Choice and Sustainability: Why Buying Local, Eating Less Meat, and Taking Baby Steps Won't Work* both written by Richard Oppenlander.

[54] Pearce, 2011. Link: http://www.hedweb.com/animals/interview.html

[55] http://www.farmforward.com/farming-forward/factory-farming

[56] Philosopher David Pearce provides the following contemplation on the substrates of suffering and their being anything but uniquely human:

> We often find it convenient to act as though the capacity to suffer were somehow inseparably bound up with linguistic ability or ratiocinative prowess. Yet there is absolutely no evidence that this is the case, and a great deal that it isn't. The functional regions of the brain which subserve physical agony, the "pain centres", and the mainly limbic substrates of emotion, appear in phylogenetic terms to be remarkably constant in the vertebrate line. The neural pathways involving serotonin, the periaquaductal grey matter, bradykinin, dynorphin, ATP receptors, the major opioid families, substance P etc all existed long before hominids walked the earth. Not merely is the biochemistry of suffering disturbingly similar where not effectively type-identical across a wide spectrum of vertebrate (and even some invertebrate) species. It is at least possible that members of any species whose members have more pain cells exhibiting greater synaptic density than humans sometimes suffer

more atrociously than we do, whatever their notional "intelligence".

Pearce, 1995/2007, p. 15.

[57] http://planetark.org/wen/57488

[58] Davies, 2011. Link:
http://www.ncbi.nlm.nih.gov/pubmed/21117987

[59] Kijlstra, Meerburg & Bos, 2009. Link:
http://www.ncbi.nlm.nih.gov/pubmed/20003752
Miranda et al., 2006 (reference found in Bohanec, 2013, p. 179).

[60] Comis, 2014. Link:
http://www.huffingtonpost.com/bob-comis/the-importance-of-our-evolution-beyond-killing-for-food_b_4518133.html

[61] See also the following link for good material, for instance some short but enlightening contemplations over "humane" farming from some former "humane" farmers themselves: http://www.humanemyth.org/.

[62] Eckel, 2008. Link:
http://ajcn.nutrition.org/content/87/4/799.short

[63] Radzevičienė & Ostrauskas, 2012. Link:
http://www.ncbi.nlm.nih.gov/pubmed/22390963

[64] Qin et al., 2007. Link:
http://www.ncbi.nlm.nih.gov/pubmed/17704029
Song et al., 2013. Link:

http://www.ncbi.nlm.nih.gov/pubmed/23256145

Chan et al., 2001. Link:

http://www.ncbi.nlm.nih.gov/pubmed/11566656

Kroenke et al., 2013. Link:

http://jnci.oxfordjournals.org/content/early/2013/03/08/jnci.djt027.abstract

[65] http://www.peacefulprairie.org/outreach/CageFree.pdf

[66] http://www.humanemyth.org/happycows.htm

BIBLIOGRAPHY

Adebamowo C. A., Spiegelman D., Danby F. W., Frazier A. L., Willett W. C., Holmes M. D. (2005). High school dietary dairy intake and teenage acne. *J Am Acad Dermatol*. 52(2), pp. 207-214. Link: http://www.ncbi.nlm.nih.gov/pubmed/15692464

Aggidis, G. et al., (2013, January). 'Global Food: Waste Not, Want Not.' *The Institution of Mechanical Engineers.* Retrieved from: http://www.imeche.org/docs/default-source/reports/Global_Food_Report.pdf?sfvrsn=0

Arterburn L. M., Oken H. A., Bailey Hall E., Hamersley J., Kuratko C. N., Hoffman J. P. (2008). Algal-oil capsules and cooked salmon: nutritionally equivalent sources of docosahexaenoic acid. *J Am Diet Assoc*. 108(7), pp. 1204-1209. Link: http://www.ncbi.nlm.nih.gov/pubmed/18589030

Babatunde, J. (2011, February). 'Livestock diseases: Africa lacks capacity for veterinary services – reports'. *Vanguard Media limited.* Retrieved from: http://www.vanguardngr.com/2011/02/livestock-diseases-africa-lacks-capacity-for-veterinary-services-reports/#sthash.RhngLYv1.dpuf

Bauer, I., Crewther, S., Pipingas, A., Sellick, L., Crewther, D. (2013). Does omega-3 fatty acid supplementation enhance neural efficiency? A review of the literature. *Hum Psychopharmacol*. Advance online publication. doi:

10.1002/hup.2370. Link:
http://www.ncbi.nlm.nih.gov/pubmed/24285504

Beezhold B. L., Johnston C. S., Daigle D. R. (2009). Preliminary evidence that vegetarian diet improves mood. Poster from: APHA 137th annual meeting and expo. Link: https://apha.confex.com/apha/137am/webprogram/Paper2 06464.html

Beezhold B. L., Johnston C. S., Daigle D. R. (2010). Vegetarian diets are associated with healthy mood states: a cross-sectional study in seventh day adventist adults. *Nutr J.* Published online: doi: 10.1186/1475-2891-9-26. Link:
http://www.ncbi.nlm.nih.gov/pubmed/20515497

Bohanec, H. & Bohanec, C. (2013). *The Ultimate Betrayal: Is There Happy Meat*. Bloomington, IN: iUniverse.

Bottemiller, H. (2011, February). 'Most U.S. Antibiotics Go to Animal Agriculture'. *Food Safety News.* Retrieved from:
http://www.foodsafetynews.com/2011/02/fda-confirms-80-percent-of-antibiotics-used-in-animal-ag/#.Us0tNPgvk8o

Chan J. M., Stampfer M. J., Ma J., Gann P. H., Gaziano J. M., Giovannucci E. (2001). Dairy products, calcium, and prostate cancer risk in the Physicians' Health Study. *Am J Clin Nutr*. 74, pp. 549-554. Link:
http://www.ncbi.nlm.nih.gov/pubmed/11566656

Charles, D. (2013, July). 'Are Antibiotics On The Farm Risky Business?'. *National Public Radio.* Retrieved from:
http://www.npr.org/blogs/thesalt/2013/07/11/200870193/are-antibiotics-on-the-farm-risky-business

Comis, B. (2014, January). 'The Importance of Our Evolution Beyond Killing for Food'. *The Huffington Post.* Retrieved from:
http://www.huffingtonpost.com/bob-comis/the-importance-of-our-evolution-beyond-killing-for-food_b_4518133.html

Consumer Reports. (2014, January). 'The high cost of

cheap chicken: 97% of the breasts we tested harbored bacteria that could make you sick. Learn how to protect yourself.' *Consumer Reports.* Retrieved from:
http://www.consumerreports.org/cro/magazine/2014/02/the-high-cost-of-cheap-chicken/index.htm

Craig, W.J., Mangels, A.R, American Dietetic Association. (2009). Position of the American Dietetic Association: vegetarian diets. *Journal of the American Dietetic Association.* 109 (7): 1266-1282. Link:
http://www.ncbi.nlm.nih.gov/pubmed/19562864

Danby F. W. (2009). Acne, dairy and cancer: The 5α-P link. *Dermatoendocrinol.* 1(1), pp. 12-16. Link:
http://www.ncbi.nlm.nih.gov/pmc/articles/PMC2715202/

Darmadi-Blackberry I., Wahlqvist M. L., Kouris-Blazos A., Steen B., Lukito W., Horie Y., Horie K. (2004). Legumes: the most important dietary predictor of survival in older people of different ethnicities. *Asia Pac J Clin Nutr.* 13(2), pp. 217-220. Link:
http://www.ncbi.nlm.nih.gov/pubmed/15228991

Davies, P. R. (2011). Intensive swine production and pork safety. *Foodborne Pathog Dis.* 8(2), pp. 189-201. Link:
http://www.ncbi.nlm.nih.gov/pubmed/21117987

Eckel, R. H. (2008). Egg consumption in relation to cardiovascular disease and mortality: the story gets more complex. *Am J Clin Nutr.* 87(4), pp. 799-800. Link:
http://ajcn.nutrition.org/content/87/4/799.short

Ellis, R. (2013, January). Could eating cheese give you diabetes? Research suggests too much of certain foods can make the body unhealthily acidic. *The Daily Mail.* Retrieved from:
http://www.dailymail.co.uk/health/article-2509674/Could-eating-cheese-diabetes-Research-suggests-certain-foods-make-body-unhealthily-acidic.html

European Food Safety Authority (2010). Results of the monitoring of non dioxin-like PCBs in food and feed. *EFSA Journal.* 8(7), pp. 1701-1736. Link:

http://www.efsa.europa.eu/en/efsajournal/pub/1701.htm

Francione, G. L. (2012, July). 'Road Kill, Abandoned Eggs, and Dumpster Diving'. *abolitionistapproach.com*. Retrived from:
http://www.abolitionistapproach.com/road-kill-abandoned-eggs-and-dumpster-diving/#.UuuHot9HcUS

Francione, G. L. & Charlton, A. E. (2013). *Eat Like You Care: An Examination of the Morality of Eating Animals*. Kentucky: Exempla Press.

Goodland, R. & Anhang, J. (2009, November/December). 'Livestock and Climate Change'. *World Watch.* Link:
http://www.worldwatch.org/files/pdf/Livestock%20and%20Climate%20Change.pdf

Grandjean, P., Hiroshi, S., Murata, K., Eto, K. (2010). Adverse Effects of Methylmercury: Environmental Health Research Implications. *Environ Health Perspect*. 118(8), pp. 1137-1145. Link:
http://www.ncbi.nlm.nih.gov/pmc/articles/PMC2920086/

Günther A. L., Karaolis-Danckert N., Kroke A., Remer T., Buyken A. E. (2010). Dietary protein intake throughout childhood is associated with the timing of puberty. *J Nutr*. 140(3), 565-571. Link:
http://www.ncbi.nlm.nih.gov/pubmed/20042466
Hammond R. A & Levine R. (2010). The economic impact of obesity in the United States. *Diabetes Metab Syndr Obes*. 3, pp. 285-295. Link:
http://www.ncbi.nlm.nih.gov/pmc/articles/PMC3047996/

Harris, S. (2010/2011). *Moral Landscape: How Science Can Determine Human Values*. New York: Free Press.

Haslam D. W. & James T. P. (2005). Obesity. *The Lancet*. 366(9492), pp. 1197-1209. Link:
http://www.thelancet.com/journals/lancet/article/PIIS0140-6736(05)67483-1/fulltext

Hoh E., Lehotay S. J., Pangallo K. C., Mastovska K., Ngo H. L., Reddy C. M., Vetter W. (2009). Simultaneous

quantitation of multiple classes of organohalogen compounds in fish oils with direct sample introduction comprehensive two-dimensional gas chromatography and time-of-flight mass spectrometry. *J Agric Food Chem*. 57(7), pp. 2653-2660. Link:
http://www.ncbi.nlm.nih.gov/pubmed/19265383

Kijlstra A., Meerburg B. G., Bos A. P. (2009). Food safety in free-range and organic livestock systems: risk management and responsibility. *J Food Prot*. 72(12), pp. 2629-2637. Link:
http://www.ncbi.nlm.nih.gov/pubmed/20003752

Knutsen S. F. (1994). Lifestyle and the use of health services. *Am J Clin Nutr*. 59(5), pp. 1171-1175. Link:
http://www.ncbi.nlm.nih.gov/pubmed/8172119

Kroenke C. H., Kwan M. L., Sweeney C., Castillo A., Caan Bette J. (2013). High-and low-fat dairy intake, recurrence, and mortality after breast cancer diagnosis. *J Natl Cancer Inst*. 105, pp. 616-623. Link:
http://jnci.oxfordjournals.org/content/early/2013/03/08/jnci.djt027.abstract

Kromhout D., de Goede J. (2014). Update on cardiometabolic health effects of ω-3 fatty acids. *Curr Opin Lipidol*. 25(1), pp. 85-90. Link:
http://www.ncbi.nlm.nih.gov/pubmed/24345990

Luppino F. S., de Wit L. M., Bouvy P. F., Stijnen T., Cuijpers P., Penninx B. W., Zitman F. G. (2010). Overweight, obesity, and depression: a systematic review and meta-analysis of longitudinal studies. *Arch Gen Psychiatry*. 67(3), 220-229. Link:
http://www.ncbi.nlm.nih.gov/pubmed/20194822

McCarty M. F. (1999). Vegan proteins may reduce risk of cancer, obesity, and cardiovascular disease by promoting increased glucagon activity. *Med Hypotheses*. 53(6), 459-485. Link:
http://www.ncbi.nlm.nih.gov/pubmed/10687887

Melnik, B. C. (2011). Evidence for acne-promoting

effects of milk and other insulinotropic dairy products. *Nestle Nutr Workshop Ser Pediatr Program.* 67, 131-145. Link:
http://www.ncbi.nlm.nih.gov/pubmed/21335995

Miranda J. M., Vazquez B. I., Fente C. A., Cepeda A., Franco C. M., Mondragon A. (2006). Bacterial resistance to antibiotics: a means of monitoring organic pork production?. *Alimentacion, Equipos y Tecnologia* 25(215), pp. 53-56.

Murata K., Weihe P., Budtz-Jørgensen E., Jørgensen P. J., Grandjean P. (2004). Delayed brainstem auditory evoked potential latencies in 14-year-old children exposed to methylmercury. *J Pediatr.* 144(2), pp. 177-183. Link:
http://www.ncbi.nlm.nih.gov/pubmed/14760257

Nachman K. E., Baron P. A., Raber G., Francesconi K. A., Navas-Acien A., Love D. C. (2013). Roxarsone, Inorganic Arsenic, and Other Arsenic Species in Chicken: A U.S.-Based Market Basket Sample. *Environ Health Perspect.* DOI:10.1289/ehp.1206245. Link:
http://ehp.niehs.nih.gov/1206245/

O'Callaghan N., Parletta N., Milte C. M., Benassi-Evans B., Fenech M., Howe P. R. (2013). Telomere shortening in elderly individuals with mild cognitive impairment may be attenuated with ω-3 fatty acid supplementation: A randomized controlled pilot study. *Nutrition.* Advance online publication. doi: 10.1016/j.nut.2013.09.013. Link:
http://www.ncbi.nlm.nih.gov/pubmed/24342530

Oppenlander, R. (2011). *Comfortably Unaware: Global Depletion and Food Responsibility.* Minneapolis, MN: Langdon Street Press.

Oppenlander, R. (2013). *Food Choice and Sustainability: Why Buying Local, Eating Less Meat, and Taking Baby Steps Won't Work.* Minneapolis, MN: Langdon Street Press distributed by Itasca Books.

Orlich M. J., Singh P. N., Sabaté J., Jaceldo-Siegl K., Fan J., Knutsen S., Beeson W. L., Fraser G. E. (2013). Vegetarian dietary patterns and mortality in Adventist Health Study 2. *JAMA Intern Med*. 173(13), 1230-1238. Link: http://www.ncbi.nlm.nih.gov/pubmed/23836264

Pan A., Sun Q., Bernstein A. M., Schulze M. B., Manson J. E., Stampfer M. J., Willett W. C., Hu F. B. (2012). Red meat consumption and mortality: results from 2 prospective cohort studies. *Arch Intern Med*. 172(7), pp. 555-563. Link: http://www.ncbi.nlm.nih.gov/pubmed/22412075

Pearce, D. (1995/2007). *The Hedonistic Imperative*. Published online at: http://www.hedweb.com/hedab.htm. PDF download: https://cl.nfshost.com/david-pearce-the-hedonistic-imperative.pdf

Pearce, D. (2011, January) 'A Would Without Suffering?' [interview]. *hedweb.com*. Retrieved from: http://www.hedweb.com/animals/interview.html

Pimentel, D. & Pimentel, M. (2003). Sustainability of meat-based and plant-based diets and the environment. *Am J Clin Nutr*. 78(suppl), pp. 660-663. Link: http://ajcn.nutrition.org/content/78/3/660S.full.pdf

Qin L., Xu J., Wang P., Tong J., Hoshi K. (2007). Milk consumption is a risk factor for prostate cancer in Western countries: evidence from cohort studies. *Asia Pac J Clin Nutr*. 16, pp. 467-476. Link: http://www.ncbi.nlm.nih.gov/pubmed/17704029

Radzevičienė L., Ostrauskas R. (2012). Egg consumption and the risk of type 2 diabetes mellitus: a case-control study. *Public Health Nutr*. 15(8), pp. 1437-1441. Link: http://www.ncbi.nlm.nih.gov/pubmed/22390963

Reuters. (2010, April). 'Grass-Fed Beef Packs A Punch To Environment'. Reuters. Retrieved from: http://planetark.org/wen/57488

Rice, P. (2005). *101 Reasons Why I'm A Vegetarian*. New York: Lantern Books

Roach, J. (2014, February). 'To feed 4 billion more, skip meat, milk and eggs, study says'. *NBC News*. Retrieved from:
http://www.nbcnews.com/science/feed-4-billion-more-skip-meat-milk-eggs-study-says-6C10848930

Rohrmann S., Linseisen J., Jakobsen M. U., Overvad K., Raaschou-Nielsen O., et al. (2011). Consumption of meat and dairy and lymphoma risk in the European Prospective Investigation into Cancer and Nutrition. *Int J Cancer*. 128(3), pp. 623-634. Link:
http://www.ncbi.nlm.nih.gov/pubmed/20473877

Sapontzis, S. (editor) (2004). *Food for Thought: The Debate over Eating Meat*. Amherst, New York: Prometheus Books.

Silbergeld E. K., Nachman K. (2008). The environmental and public health risks associated with arsenical use in animal feeds. *Ann N Y Acad Sci*. 1140, pp. 346-357. Link:
http://www.ncbi.nlm.nih.gov/pubmed/18991934

Simon, D. (2013). *Meatonomics: How the Rigged Economics of Meat and Dairy Make You Consume Too Much-and How to Eat Better, Live Longer, and Spend Smarter*. San Francisco, CA: Conari Press.

Singh P. N., Sabaté J., Fraser G. E. (2003). Does low meat consumption increase life expectancy in humans? *Am J Clin Nutr*. 78(3) pp. 526-532. Link:
http://ajcn.nutrition.org/content/78/3/526S.long

Song Y., Chavarro J. E., Cao Y., Qiu W., Mucci L. et al. (2013). Whole milk intake is associated with prostate cancer-specific mortality among U.S. male physicians. *J Nutr*. 143, pp. 189-196. Link:
http://www.ncbi.nlm.nih.gov/pubmed/23256145

Steinfeld, H. et al. (2006). 'Livestock's Long Shadow'. *The Food and Agriculture Organization of the United Nations*. Link:
http://www.fao.org/docrep/010/a0701e/a0701e00.htm

Stokstad, E. (2014). Ammonia Pollution From Farming May Exact Hefty Health Costs. *Science*. 343(6168), p. 238. Link: http://www.sciencemag.org/content/343/6168/238.summary

Tavernise, S. (2013, September). 'Antibiotic-Resistant Infections Lead to 23,000 Deaths a Year, C.D.C. Finds'. *The New York Times.* Retrieved from: http://www.nytimes.com/2013/09/17/health/cdc-report-finds-23000-deaths-a-year-from-antibiotic-resistant-infections.html?_r=0

Tetrick, J. [Hampton Creek Foods]. (2013, June). The Future of Food [TED-talk given at TEDx Edmonton 2013]. Retrieved from: http://www.youtube.com/watch?v=RbNw00V26pw

Tonstad S., Butler T., Fraser G. E. (2009). Type of Vegetarian Diet, Body Weight, and Prevalence of Type 2 Diabetes. *Diabetes Care.* 32(5), pp. 791-796. Link: http://www.ncbi.nlm.nih.gov/pmc/articles/PMC2671114/

Trove. (2013, December). 'New Report: Chicken Is the Filthiest Meat You're Eating'. *trove.com.* Retrieved from: http://trove.com/me/content/Gv4jd

Vergnaud A. C., Norat T., Romaguera D., Mouw T., May A. M. et al. (2010). Meat consumption and prospective weight change in participants of the EPIC-PANACEA study. *Am J Clin Nutr.* 92(2), pp. 398-407. Link: http://www.ncbi.nlm.nih.gov/pubmed/20592131

Zeilmaker M. J., Hoekstra J., van Eijkeren J. C., de Jong N., Hart A., Kennedy M., Owen H., Gunnlaugsdottir H. (2013). Fish consumption during child bearing age: a quantitative risk-benefit analysis on neurodevelopment. *Food Chem Toxicol.* 54, pp. 30-34. Link: http://www.ncbi.nlm.nih.gov/pubmed/22079313

6084446R00074

Printed in Great Britain
by Amazon.co.uk, Ltd.,
Marston Gate.